Saturn's Rings

by
Jessica Roberts

Bloomington, IN      Milton Keynes, UK

authorHOUSE®

AuthorHouse™
1663 Liberty Drive, Suite 200
Bloomington, IN 47403
www.authorhouse.com
Phone: 1-800-839-8640

AuthorHouse™ UK Ltd.
500 Avebury Boulevard
Central Milton Keynes, MK9 2BE
www.authorhouse.co.uk
Phone: 08001974150

First published by AuthorHouse 8/7/2006

ISBN: 1-4259-4588-0 (sc)

Printed in the United States of America
Bloomington, Indiana

This book is printed on acid-free paper.

TABLE OF CONTENTS

MORGUE

Working at Donte Hospital, wasn't an easy task. We received children daily on the unit. Most of them were children of the streets who had been killed in gang wars, or ones who had suffered from traumatic abuse. Innocent children confused lonely and victims. A child had been shot to death in an alley over a sweater. His body lay cold on a metal slab. As I look at his body, I saw pain past his gunshot wounds.

His legs were scarred, welts maybe two months old. On his ribs were burns from hair curlers, or some kind of hot rod. There were a lot of sores and cuts on his feet and hands. As I turned the child's body over I saw four healed stab wounds. The child had obviously been abused and or a victim of the street.

Once we established identification on the child, the story became clearer. He was abused. Social services information read the child had been admitted to the hospital numerous times for abuse issues. Most of the wounds afflicted were from his parents. Social Services would take him out of the home and return him in a short period of time. He was a young runaway barely twelve years old. Forced out on the streets, escaping a home he feared even more came to a deadly end.

His final visit to the hospital would be to the morgue. Though his problems and worries were over, I could not help but to think about what he would have become, had not death found him on the streets.

A CRY UNANSWERED

Caps was a regular at the Juvenile Detention Center. He was twelve years old and had a rap sheet dating back, when he was eight. He had been arrested for stealing, burglary, robbery and drugs. This time caps was arrested for murder.

His mother and step father were both crack addicts. Caps was poor and a victim of society and abuse. His step father was the abuse in the home. Caps and the other children had visible scars and bruises. They had been abused there entire lives, and had to stay in that home to face there abuser everyday.

Caps said that he had gotten into a fight with his "step father" about 2:00am. His step father had pushed his mother down a flight of stairs, and then started to beat and kick her. When Caps tried to help her, he tried to beat Caps too. Caps said, he ran in the kitchen and grabbed a knife; then he stabbed his stepfather six times in the chest. The stab wounds were fatal. He died on the floor.

Police picked Caps up from a friend's house, charged and arrested him.

Caps and abused and neglected child; fought his abuser and it ended up fatal. Caps felt that stabbing his stepfather was the only way out for him and his family. We would have to leave it up to the state to decide his future.

NEVER SAW HIM AGAIN

Broken jaws and cans of chowder
all the fights just getting louder
wakes me up all the thru the night
why'd my mom have to be his wife

leave her be I said one night
pacing in a frantic fright
left hand carrying my rifle tight
"please don't shoot son I'm alright"

I have to stand and become a man
choice is made there was no plan
today my step dad life will end
this is where our lives begin

No more gauze
no more tape
no more beatings
no more rape
no more loosing
we will win
one thing I'm sure of in my sin
he'll never hit my mom again.

NOTIFY HIS NEXT OF KIN

A child from trauma
Roll him in
Newfangled life
A fatal end
In his pocket
Was letter
come back home
when things get better
the letter read
he had to go
she made a choice
another joe
hell find a job
out on the streets
stay clear of danger
he may meet
its time for you to be a man
what I'd tell you bout the band
this is where your life begins.

JUST A RUB

Dripping wet, with chlorine water,
anxious girl to see her father.
lounging in a pool side chair,
he pulls me close so we could share.
just a rub against my bottom,
underneath the cartoon towel.
it's my dad so it's o.k.,
he'll only rub me light today.
he rubs my chest and nipples light,
position my body so it's right.
slid his fingers thru my walls,
a teardrop was my only call.
I'm sorry princess, be on your way
that's enough for you today.

I'LL JUST WALK

Trying to make it to my friend's house cross town, I jumped on my old ten speed bike. Hot and sweaty I stopped by the store for a drink. I came out of the store and my bike was gone.

I started walking. A car pulled up on the side of me, a lady asked did I need a ride. I said "yes". I jumped into the care and we pulled off. She asked me could she touch me as she slid her hands on my private. I was completely frozen. My guess she was trying to make it hard. I was completely nervous. Then the lady stopped the car and asked could she suck it. I said "no". I jumped out of the car and started running towards my friend's house. I ran all the way there.

I told my friend's mom what had happened. We looked around for the car, to see if the lady had followed me and so that we could give the police a good description, of her and the car. The lady was gone. My friend's mother told me to never get a ride from anyone again. My friend and I both agreed that we would just walk.

<u>NOT THIS TIME</u>

Walking home thru the alley,
grocery bags an empty belly
heard a voice said stop right there,
out the shadows he appeared
big and tall,
dressed in black
says "do you need help with your bags",
I told him "please don't come any closer"
he says "don't tell me how to approach you",
he voice was deep, he showed no fear
my legs were shaking, I dropped a tear,
a sign of strength a women's cry
not knowing someone's about to die,
he moves in slowly I stand my ground
position my body,
there's no one else around.

I reach for my pistol,
looked in his eyes
fired two shots and said,
"not this time".

I DIDN'T SAY YES EITHER

Never wanted the drink
I drunk anyway,
didn't want the weed
we smoke today,
should have pop the pills
we took in the car,
couldn't pass up
the trip to the bar,
given the acid so I thought I try
cocaine past around ,
I'll snort me a line
everyone's happy,
that means I am too
time for some mushrooms,
though I should be thru
he asked me for sex,
or was it a show
I didn't say yes,
and I couldn't say "no".

PRAYER WORKS

My father was a pastor of a church down south. My dead was mean, yet quiet. He suffered from a mental illness that would cause him to flare from the slightest annoyance. My mother had been dead for some years. When I was eighteen years old, I had gotten pregnant with my daughter. My father got upset and thru me out of the house.

The streets were killing me. Twenty-three years old, homeless with a five year old daughter. I had also developed a drug addiction from an ex-boyfriend. With no energy, no money, I found myself on my fathers doorstep.

My father told me that my daughter could not live inside of his house. He said he had a place for her. He walked me out back, in the old cellar, I called a dungeon. I could remember the place from when I was young. For punishment father would keep me there for days. He told me this is where my daughter would have to live. I followed fathers' orders.

I could still hear her crying and screaming for me not to leave her. Everyday, three times a day; I place food at the top of the stairs for weeks. I would stare out of the window at the dungeon, praying for my daughter that I could not help.

One Sunday morning I took her breakfast, and her dinner was on the top of the stairs. Picking up the plate I walked slowly down the steps of the dungeon. My daughter was lying there silent. Her lips were chapped and blistered. Her small body was frail, and limp, she was not breathing. I sat on the floor rocking her body in my arms, singing the same spirituals I sung as a victim of the dungeon. I was glad she didn't have to suffer anymore pain.

FOOTBALL TEAM

We were reigning champions of the state. High school football was the town's favorite pastime. I was a cheerleader in my freshman year. On our away games, we would stay over at a hotel. We had chaperons though we would sneak out of the room at night.

On of the nights an older player called me into his room. He introduced his self to me as the quarterback. There was another guy in the room with him. I cane in and sat down on the bed. He asked me did I want to have sex I said "no". He laid me back on the bed anyway, pulled my panties off and pushed his penis inside of me. The other guy came over and stuck his penis into my mouth. They switch places and went back and forth for about 30 minutes. Afterwards they let me out of the room.

When we came back in town the next evening there was a parade of people gathered around the school bus. We had won our championship game. The team was happy. The town was happy. I didn't say a word about what had happened to me.

UNDERSTAND ME

Almost to my apartment building
coming home from church that evening,
singing spirituals, holy light
guide me on my path tonight.

Angels with me all the way
keeps me safe,
I walk and pray.

As I walk, a man stepped out,
he startled me, I opened my mouth
the blood of Jesus is what came out.
the blood of Jesus I said again
the blood of Jesus and that man ran.

CAMPING TRIP

Boys scout camping trip was annual every summer. Two adults and six boys would go in the woods and camp for the weekend. We would usually camp in the woods near the picnic area. This time we went deeper into the woods. We played games during the day, roasted marshmallows in the pit as we told ghost stories thru the night.

About 1:00 in the morning, one of the scout leaders came into my tent and told me to take off my clothes, and get on my knees. When I did, that's when he put his penis into my mouth. He started moving it all around. I was crying. He took his penis out of my mouth and started rubbing it with his hands until semen came out. He put the semen all over my face and rubbed it with his penis. Afterwards he told me to go to the out house and wash my face, I did.

When I came back to the tent he was gone. The next morning, I went on as if nothing had happened. I never told my parents or anyone about the trip. I never thought about that night again.

DIED INSIDE

My father on my sixteenth birthday
said there was something he would like to say
first he gave me a diamond ring
"I love you no matter how weird this seems"
after a hug, he took my hand
you have to see me as a man
I'm going to lay in the bed with you
thee is something I would like to do
don't be frighten it's just sex
when I'm finished you can rest
I said I never done this before
it wont hurt it may be sore
mom's in bed sleeping well
she wont know if you don't tell
quiet is how we have to keep it
just our little private secret

Had a secret of my own
I let him find out on his own
the one thing he lost was my respect
never told him I had sex
wasn't a virgin, I couldn't hide
he knew it when, he died inside.

THIS TIME I LIED

Went to a party
Met up with up with this guy
We went in the room
He threw me on the bed
I reached for the door
He stole my purse
He beat me up
Must have been drugged
I called the police
I said I was raped
This time he was arrested
This time he went to jail
This time I lied.

DRUGGED AND RAPED

Four of us we all went out
Skirts and pumps
A lighter route.
in a charming friendly way
compliment me on my braids
conversation hype I think
he must have slipped one in my drink
didn't feel myself leave
woke up in a pile of leaves
broken glass under my feet
cracked my jaw, my ribs, my teeth.

Suffered from a brutal beating
guess it was only death I cheated,
vaginal and anal rape
lucky I'm alive today
left inside to contemplate
kill myself or should I stay.

I THINK SO

I asked him did he touch her
he replied, I told you no
she doesn't even talk to me
How will I ever know?
her hips are getting wider
and she's discharging a different scent
they sleep together all the time
does not look innocent
I want to ask her she might shell
just a talk I won't yell
sometimes she sad, some clues will tell
eye contact will break a snail
my line of questioning
brings a sigh
"what are you asking me and why"?
I just want to be apart of your life
if something is wrong we'll make it right
she won't talk and he can't hide
he won't break and I can't slide
she won't show what's absorbed inside
victimized in front of my eyes

PREGNANT AND HOMELESS

I was fifteen years old when I had gotten pregnant. I was living with my mom in a homeless shelter called "our mission". It was hot we had no shower, only a sink to share with my little sister, mother, and her new husband. My mother had been evicted out of the apartment, so the shelter was the only place we could stay.

An HRS worker came to the shelter one day and referred me to a place called Keta. Keta was a shelter for pregnant and homeless women and girls. Keta was ran by Christian women who were strict on curfew, diet, and education. At Keta we were able to receive our proper benefits, education and meals. We attended, parenting classes, Lamaze classes, school, games, and everything to keep us busy and healthy during the pregnancy.

Keta made my situation the best it could have possibly been. I was birth educated, found friends, routes and alternatives. I was comfortable and glad to be around loving people in a safe atmosphere. I was healthy; my son was healthy and I owed it all to the people who helped me at Keta.

WHEN I GROW UP

I spread my legs when men walk by
touch their crotch
bat my eyes
sex is what I rather do
vaginal and anal too
talk a lot exotic toys
love men women and boys
sex with objects, sex with kin
if you want I'll sex your friends
my parents alone taught me this
how to tongue
with a kiss
breaded for a life of sex and money
molded into the common dummy
promiscuities
spoils and strife
unanswered prayers for a better life

UNCLE LARRY'S SUMMER HOME

Uncle Larry has a beach house located directly on the beach. My younger brother and I went to visit him for a week. When we first arrived, he showed us our rooms and the rest of the house. The beach was next. Everyday Uncle Larry allowed us to play on the beach while he did stuff around the house.

Uncle Larry called me in one day from playing. He said he wanted to take pictures. Uncle Larry told me to take off my clothes and lay on the bed. He told me to open my legs and put my hands on my breast. Then he started to take pictures. Next he told me to bend over and touch my toes. I could feel his hand on my bottom and I could here the flashing off the camera. When Uncle Larry took off his clothes, the tears I was holding begin to flow really hard and steadily. I believe he was about to rape me, then someone came thru the door. The door slammed closed. My uncle jumped up. My brother had scared him. He hurried up and put on his clothes, while I lay on the bed naked and shaking. Uncle Larry looked at me and said "hurry up and put on your clothes, we will finish this some other time."

My brother had stopped Uncle Larry from raping me. Tears dried up, I could breath. I didn't understand why Uncle Larry wanted to take pictures of me, or anything else. The rest of the week I was quiet. I felt lonely and betrayed. All I had with me was my brother. The love I had for my Uncle had now turned into fear.

WARD OF THE STATE

My aunt had custody of me and four more of my mother's children. We were begging to be unbearable. We spent most of our time on the streets. We were street kids. My aunt called social services and we became wards of the state. Throughout the years we have all been split up in different foster homes. The lady that owned the home would beat all the children with fan cords. The welts would either be gone or covered by the time school or social services came around. One time she hit me so hard I fell out of a third story window and broke my arm. I was taken out of that home.

The next home was worse. I lived with "Papa Mann" and his wife. He was mean, however, she was meaner. They would have parties, socials they would call it. It would only be me and three other girls that were placed in the home. We were made to dance naked and have sex with each other. We would have to use toys and other objects, anything they wanted to see.

Once his wife came into the room with a bottle. She told me tonight it would only be us. His wife asked me to bed over and put my hands on the wall. When I looked back, she was sticking the bottle in my anus. The bottle hurt me really bad. When I asked her to stop, she just kept shoving and pushing. After about 10 minutes of raping me, she stopped, thru the bottle at me and walked out of the room. She didn't say a word about how I felt, never did.

I went to sleep thinking about how my life would be if I went to another foster home. Would it be better or worse? My bones were not broken, though my body was still sore. Will I still be in pain?

FRESH ALREADY

The clinic had been located in the same area for years. One of the floors in the building had been dedicated specifically for sexual transmitted diseases.

During the summer a lot of children ages eleven thru sixteen wee infected with the H.I.V virus and other STD's. We held classes with the youth on condom safety and educated them on birth control and prevention.

There were twelve year old girls pregnant. Some of these father's of the children were as young as thirteen and as old forty five maybe older. Some of them were victims of incest. These kids were infected with diseases that they would have for the rest of their lives.

Some of these children acquired these unsafe sexual habits at home. Victims of abuse, neglect, even child prostitution. These were children who have been exposed or included in adult sex acts. Most of the children reported when they acquired new infections; some of them were too ashamed to be repeatedly seen at the doctor, the same with adults.

As the years go by the children are still at risk of being infested with STD's or repeated pregnancy; also becoming less aware of birth control and prevention. It is important to keep these programs in operation. Children, who have not been educated, have a greater chance of repeating the cycle of infections and diseases.

BREAK THE CYCLE

My grandfather was a drunk. He spent most of his time drinking and cursing. It would always start out verbal and then get physical. Most of the time he would hit, and yell at my father; then my father would take it out on me. My father treated me the same way, my grandfather treated him.

He'd beat me with empty bottles. Sometimes he would throw them at me. The worse thing he ever did was; got drunk and hit me in the face with an old gin bottle. He broke half of my face.

My upper lip was split in half. My eye had two veins busted in it, and my nose was broken. I lay dazed on the floor bleeding from my head and face. My face was swollen, I was missing two teeth and he was still beating me.

Abuse went on. We lived thru a cycle of hatred and alcoholism. My father and grandfather were both angry men. They both buried there problems with alcohol and ruled with an iron fist.

I promised myself that I would never become an alcoholic. In order to break the cycle of abuse, I would have to eliminate the biggest problem.

GIFT AND THE CURSE

Born in power, fortune and fame,
toot my nose up on the way.
don't care how you feel today,
some bodies matter, it's been that way.
don't change a thing for me,
just that is blue, and I like green.
I live my parent's identity,
and I know there is somewhere you have to be.
flashing cameras, start the show,
it's my choice where we will go,
don't ask me I'll let you know.
dark is frowned on even me,
darker secrets fortune brings.
friends of family, made my own,
never lonely when alone.
drugs and parties, high all night,
we do what we want,
cause that's what's right.
money glamour, media hype,
I guess I'll live my parent's life.

FAULTLESS INFECTIONS

My family and I moved closer to the hospital in which my grandson had lived. His situation had become really bad and needed family close. He was born with full blown AIDS. He also had a spinal cord infection. The doctors moved him from a local hospital to a treatment center for children. All of the children there needed more that a year worth of recovery. His body was breaking down; sue to him fighting off infections. A few months into his stay, both his parents had died. They both had aids.

My grandson's body had developed and he had begun to gain weight. His infection was accepting the medication, despite the virus. We stayed in the same city as my grandson, so that we could see him everyday. Each day we take a larger step closer to completing his healing process and recovery. I promise my daughter I would stay by his side as I was with her.

MINITURE CHALK TRACE

My daughter was three months old when I killed her. One evening my wife was at work, I was alone with our three month old baby. The baby would not stop crying. Every time I would watch her she would cry all thru the night. I was In the middle of a football game and she had started crying.

I walked in the back room, picked her up out of the crib and started to shake her. I was so mad; I was yelling and screaming for her to shut up. I just kept shaking her and shaking her, until her small body slipped out of my hands and on to the floor. I froze.

My brother came in the room yelling what happened. My daughter lay on the floor stiff and dead. I had shaken her to death. My heart felt like it stopped beating. I could not breathe; I was dizzy, throwing up, total disbelief. There was no more crying, screaming, just silence. I had realized I killed my daughter.

SHATTERED INNOCENCE

I worked a story once, suburb area near highway 13. A call forwarded to my cell phone about an infant rape. I can remember the scene full of police officers, the family, news crews and neighbors. A mother had been killed, a baby had been raped and the father was suspected of committing the crimes.

A mother came home to her infant daughter being raped. The mother was raped and beaten then strangled to death. A neighbor had heard noise then called the police. The baby was found on the living room floor next to her mother alive; however she had been raped. Only four months into this world, it was a tragic story.

After an investigation the father was arrested and convicted of infant rape and murder. I followed the story to the end hoping that he would be sentenced to death. He was. Though these stories happen all around the world I have not actually seen a rape and murder as vicious as these. The outcome was satisfying.

Though there was nothing that could be done to replace the family that was lost we could bring them justice. The father was ultimately sentenced to his death.

CHILD RAPE

Easter Sunday last year we were all at the parks Easter egg hunt. The kids were scattered all around the park, looking for eggs. Once the bell rung the children were to meet under the tent. There was one boys missing, ten year old Mike Mays. A police search was called after about twenty minutes of searching. He was found dead in a bush nearby.

There was a gash in the center of his head and his pants were pulled below his knees. He had been raped. His throat was cut and he was left in a bush to die. Police said, "He had been hit with a blunt object." He died on the scene. The child's family, close friends and the community cried for the police to hurry and catch the killer.

June came quickly and there was another murder. A young boy age eleven had been killed coming home from school. His body was found on a bank of a nearby river. He had been also bashed in and his throat was cut. The town knew that we had someone stalking and preying on young boys.

Two weeks later the killer was found and arrested. By catching this killer the town was able to put behind us certain fear for our children. We came together and have been diligently working on crime prevention and protecting our children.

LIFE OF THE PARTY

I was invited to a college rave one night by a couple of guys, so I decided to go. The party was packed with a lot of young people, light, drugs and guys the usual party. Walking around the frat house, I saw different things going on in the rooms.

As I entered a room, one of the guys offered me a line of cocaine, I did it. Then they offered me ecstasy pills and I took them too. I felt good. We were doing drugs and feeling the music.

I sat on the table and started playing with myself. I was taking off my clothes feeling the drugs. The guys that were in the room started to take of their clothes. One started to put his penis in my mouth and the other guy put his penis in my vagina. I was enjoying it; they wanted anal sex, so we did it. They were hard and rough I was numb and high.

I woke up the next morning realizing what I had done. I had regrets of course. It was the drugs. I was completely overtaken by the feeling. I had gone all out without even realizing a thing, only being the life of the party.

STARTED OFF DANCING

Viper Strip Club was a real hell hole. I started off dancing there when I was sixteen years old. My mother abandoned me when I was twelve, been with my dad every since. My father was a rapist, I was a teenage runaway. I spent most of my time with older women hanging in the club. Cash came quick. I went to work thru the week and the weekends. About two months into dancing, I developed a cocaine habit, which ultimately doubled, then tripled; eventually it spent out of control. I couldn't see any of my money. One of the girls told me I could get extra money doing private shows. I took her offer.

I worked shows, prostituted, hotels, and parties. I even start working the streets. My habit spent me into a life of more drugs, sex, porn movies, films, and a never ending cycle of misery. At one point of time, I had sold every thing in my house including my clothes and my car. Half of the time I was so high, I couldn't move. My weight had dropped down to almost 90 pounds. My lips were cracked; my eyes were bulging due to my face being sunk in. I was eighteen years old with a razor blade to my wrist. I drowned in more drugs. I had taken so many pills and snorted so much cocaine, I collapsed. I woke up three says later in a hospital bed. I had cut myself as well as overdosed.

The place was called squares of care. It was a mental and rehabilitation clinic. The doctor thought I should stay in the hospital to seek treatment. Part of my rehabilitation was to talk with a counselor. How I had so far ruined my life with drugs and alcohol. We also talked about my father raping me and my mother leaving. After we made contact with my grandparents they supported me thru my stay. I lived in the hospital for almost two years. I was given a second chance at life. I was completely rehabilitated, both mentally and physically. I was now living both a healthy and responsible life.

IT WAS THE DRUGS

Anal rape the police called it
can't remember past the party
drugs in season, open closet
blurry faces, when I recall it
try to focus on a face
how did I get there?
where's the plate?

Cocaine smeared across my nose,
Grim and dirt between my toes
remember the lights, the feel of the floor,
sex in the air, reach for the door
gasping for air, heart pounding with fear,
voices are heard, someone is near
help me; I can't feel a thing,
my body is weak, my throat is in pain
my mind is all reckless,
I'm feeling no shame.

END RESULT

As a convicted felon in prison sentenced to die; life for me seemed as if it was messed up from the start. I was born inside a prison facility and became a ward of the state. Raised in the boys and home and different foster families, I ran into a lot of abusive situations. I was raped by a man name "Big Joe", he was a foster dad. Joe raped all the boys in the home. He would beat us with ash trays and bottles all day. When night fall came he would have sex with us as if we were women. We weren't. We wee young boys being anal raped.

When I was thirteen years of age I ran away. I turned into a life of crime. By age twenty five I had already did two prison terms. I was ruthless. I was a killer, robber, rapist, and drug dealer; worse of all I felt I had a reason to be angry and violent. My anger for my foster family had spilled across the streets of the United States. I was a violent child, violent teen, and a violent man.

The last job I did was a murder robbery. I needed money fast; I killed two store clerks as I tried to rob and convenience store. During the robbery I was shot. I was down again.

I am currently sentenced to die. All of my wrong doings were and result of living an abused life. Looking for vengeance and answers to poverty, I found prison and captivity. I now face my death.

LETS FIGHT

Scared are you?
you should be,
I don't want anyone
touching me,
don't talk to me
leave me alone,
it's just me on my own
no witnesses,
no witnesses
crime on my mind,
won't be a victim
to no one this time,
have my weapon
my gun and knife,
he will pay for raping me that night
I am angry and vengeful beware of my wrath,
I'm taking it personal
I'm leaving him dead.

IM JUST SAYING

I'm just saying I need some space
my mind is dark
emotionally erased
the chip on my shoulder
has the gun in your face
my hand in your pocket
the clip on my waste
cant help that I'm angry
been pacing this route
no mind over matter
no other way out

Burdened with problems
I'm bringing it to you
I say what I mean
it's all known to be true
call me repulsive, I get quite absurd,
unpleasant and foul mouthed
I mean every word

Life or death is the option I'm weighing,
a cost for a vengeful life I'm paying.

DRUGS

I've been on drugs for ten years. I started smoking pot at age eleven. I grew up in an abusive home. My father, a drug dealer and user turned me on to stronger drugs as I got older. I was fourteen years old on cocaine and acid. We both used cocaine on a regular basis; until we tried rocks. Smoking rocks really took control of our lives. We started doing robberies. Robbing the neighborhood, stores, churches, anywhere we could find money or something valuable to feed our habit. We turned to a life a crime, drugs, and murder.

Eventually I was sixteen years old using heroin. Heroin was worse than crack; I spent more money, committed more crimes. One night we both were on heroin, and were going to do another robbery. This time we just went in the store shooting. We grabbed purses, wallets and everything we could get of value and left; people were dead. All I knew at that time is that I had my money for my drugs and I was high. I lay there with a needle in my arm. The heroin had me bitter and I didn't even care.

Weeks after the robbery, my dad had died on an overdose of heroin. I sat in a chair next to his body and just starred at him. I couldn't cry for him either. For the rest of that evening, I continued shooting up, almost as if I wanted to kill myself. My body had gone completely numb. I had committed murders and now my father was dead; there was nothing left for me but space, drugs, and death.

SUBSTANCE ABUSE

MARIJUANA mellowed back,
joints and blunts I roll them fat.

COCAINE eats inside my nose,
however it keeps me on my toes.

EXTASY'S up's and downs are loose,
inhale vapors, orange juice.

MUSHROOMS dazes strong as the pasture
flashing lights and echoed laughter.

ACID SHEETS I go for trips
climb the wall, with cartoon grips.

HERION leaves me with a twitch
needle tracks, have left there prints.

CRACKROCK beams me for a minute
beauty queens me for a minute

ALCOHOL my favorite chaser
with my drugs, ass lemon flavors.

As my day turn to evening, evening turn to day
since I don't have a favorite
I'll take all of them today.

MY FAVORITE PUNISHMENT

My grandmother was a bitter old lady. There were ten of us under her thumb, or under her house I should say. She believed in strong, mean discipline. Some reason grandma liked to beat us, maybe because our mother was nowhere to be found. My mother dropped us off about four years ago and never returned. My mother had six children.

We lived under grandmother's house for four years. She would come down to the basement with the same weapons every night. She had a cord, stick, whip or strap.

She would tie us to a chair and beat us with whatever was chosen. The pain lasted for hours. Sometimes the beating would tear our skin.

We hated grandma. All we could do was hate her. We believed grandma saw us as our mother's burdened. She hated us. Therefore our lives were cold and miserable. With nothing left except broken bones and dreams, we would sit in the basement and wait on the say our mother returned.

GOOD OLE DAYS

Bitter days of lather soap,
hand tightly gripped across my throat
scalding water, blistered burns,
gain, green, greener than the ferns
bruised and battered sore and raw,
marked the children raised by pa.

eat of the floor three meals a day,
girls sleep in the bed, he have his way
raped and beaten,
unable to talk
marked the children raised by pa.

trapped inside a cold dark cell,
he made our lives a living hell
broken pride and helpless pleads,
there wasn't one good day for me.

MY SISTER TOO

It was a Saturday night. My dad had a card game and invited a few of his friends over. My mom was at work, as usual on card nights. It sounded like a party. There was a lot of music and a lot of noise. My sister and I were in the back room down the hallway. We both eventually fell asleep.

Late in the evening, I could hear the door crack open. I saw a man come in and shut the door. He came over to my bed and put his hand over my mouth. I tried to yell, he put the pillow over my head. He pulled up my night gown and raped me. All I can remember was trying to move he was on top of me like weights.

My step dad came in the room and grabbed him off of me. I was in the room a long time, until the police came. My mom came home shortly after. My step dad was talking to the police and my mom; after they talked we went to the hospital.

My parents apologized for what happen to me that night, and assured me that it would never happen again. I'm glad I'm alive my sister, who was in the same room is alive, and we are able to heal and move on with our lives.

HE RAN OUT

Lied to
cheated on
Broken up
Lonely
Hopeless
Fondled
Belittled
Distressed
Raped
Neglected
Disheveled
Doubted
Careless
Beaten
Unwilled
Limp
Poisoned
Abused
Abandoned
Forgotten
Left

LEFT BEHIND

My family consists of me, my two little brothers and my mom. Mom was and alcoholic. Mom would get drunk and like to fight her children. She would always pull my hair and punch me real hard in the face. I thought it was the alcohol, though she would only hit me; never my brothers. Sometimes she would wake me in the middle of the night and order me to take off my clothes. Mom would beat me with extension cords till blood poured out off my legs and arms.

My room was the closet inside of her bedroom. I stayed in there until she was ready to beat me. She would often tie me to the bed and throw nick nacs at my face and chest. Thru the years I suffered from physical, verbal, mental abuse and neglect. If she had stop drinking things would have gotten better. I could not wait for that day. I ran.

I ended up in a church home for runaway teenagers. Sometimes I think about my brothers, hoping that she would not beat them, now that I am gone. Maybe she had stop drinking, that would have stop the hatred. I often worry about my future including my younger brothers, though I fear the life I left behind.

SAME SONG

Trapped inside my childhood days,
the things dad did and called it play
he hurt us in so many ways,
talk of freedom to much to say.

Mom could never say too much,
routinely cringing at his touch
sober days a mouth of malt,
alternative end already sought.

Thinking of who I'll leave behind,
a younger reflection of my tribe
my mother's tears have stained my soul,
her past is now my life at home.

Has my tears bruised my siblings heart,
blood stained sheets lifeless marks
cold and hardened, bitter assault,
I'm ready to take my final walk.

I can't leave my sister,
behind and alone
to be lost in the tune of my same song,
mom's to discouraged
she can't be strong,
when she awakes
we'll both be gone.

QUEEN BEE

Bee was a Rican from the Bronx. A twenty-eight year old pimp. Bee was a runaway, originally from a small town in Texas. Her father had been sexually abusing her since she was 10 years old. Bee's father was a rapist. The family knew of him and everything he did; no one ever did anything about it. He was a mean cold man. Home wasn't the place to be. Bee was sixteen years old when she finally ran away from home, and ended up on the cold streets of New York.

Bee was country, though fast paced. As soon as she hit the streets, she started making money. Bee held down her apartment with three other girls, she had met on the streets. The girls were a little slower, so she hooked them on to the game. Once bee had built up her girls and her cliental, a lot of money was coming in. With the money she was making she was able to afford brand new cars, clothes and a better place to live. Then she got into drugs.

Bee was pimping working and selling drugs. Things were going this way for years. Bee practically owned a hotel especially for her girls and her clients. Under the table, she owned a few of them. Bee kept the girls because she was nice to them and always gave them a fair share of their money. The ladies were clean, the drugs and money was right; bee had it all.

Other people who needed to make money on the streets did not like the way Bee ran the streets. Bee owned it all. Bee was pretty, fine, Rican and rich off the money she had made on the streets.

One late night coming out of her hotel building, she was shot one single time in the head. Her body lay lifeless on the city concrete. A crowd surrounded her as she took her last breath. Bee had been killed because of her street status. Queen Bee's memory will always be in the hearts of her girls, her tricks, and her streets.

TRAIL BLAZA

Sixteen years old I ran away from home,
the streets I did not plane to roam
New York, New York big city of dreams,
escape your life and fulfill your needs.

A need to feel you serve a purpose
there's more to life than what is on commercial,
instead of my dreams I found the street
a life of hitchhiking,
a life of deceit.

I picked up my habits throughout the states,
drained the needles, cleaned the plates
hiked across the highway miles,
aging body, lonely child
kicked the dust of desert plains,
lost and forgotten, cast away
where will my meal come from today,
prostitution my only way.

Maybe I'll find a place to lay,
cardboard box or stacks of hay
searching for meaning in a life unknown,
the life of a trail blaza is now my own.

NOWHERE TO GO

All I know is that I wanted to run. My trouble started when my mother remarried. All of a sudden her kids became a problem. We were her kids from her last marriage at least that's what we were called. It was almost as if she had forgotten she ever loved us. He would beat us, while she sits high, smoking cigarettes and snorting cocaine.

We would stand in the corner for hours at a time. He would make us urinate on ourselves just so that he could have an excuse to beat us. One he got a bat and broke my brother's rib cage, mom tried to stop him; it was pointless. We wanted out. We didn't know how to run away. Where to run? Where to hide? All we knew is that if we stayed, we would end up like my brother, even worse, my mother.

I would have to stay and fight for my brother and my mother. He beat mom too. Only mom would cry al night and we couldn't help her. When my brother got out the hospital and came home, we said no more abuse. We called the police and he went to jail. After he went to jail, we moved to another city and sate. We had our mom back and she had her life and her children.

BIG CIGARETTES

Our new step father didn't like us from the start. My mom had my brothers and I from a previous marriage. My stepfather believed that we were sneaky and deserved to be punished. It wasn't that, we just weren't his boys. He would lock us in the closet with huge cigars, at that time we called them big cigarettes. He would let the cigars burn all the way down until the smoke filled the closet.

When he would get upset he would burn us on the legs and hands with the cigars. Our step father enjoyed burning us. We were either being burned with the cigars or our eyes were burning from the smoke. We hated our step father, though there was nothing we could do, we took it one day at a time.

Things were better once we were older and got out of the house. The memories of my stepfather, the closet and the cigars, no longer hurts me.

NO KIDS PLEASE

I promise that I love you,
but your kids must leave
I said I would provide,
though I don't want them please.

we can travel around the world,
though your kids must leave
I know I can make you happy,
I cant help them please
my heart belongs to you,
though your kids must leave
our fire is still burning,
so no kids please.

OUR FAMILY SECRET

My father raised six girls by himself. All of us became successful ladies. Me being the oldest, I have seen it all. Growing up with my father wasn't easy. Our family was popular and we had a reputation. Education, church, and good jobs were my father's goals. We achieved the good grades, jobs, church and what people thought was a loving home. We were known as good people.

My father was a nice guy, funny and never remarried after my mother's death. In the public eye we were a flawless family. At home there were family problems. Serious issues.

Our life consisted of incest rape, sexual molestation and mental abuse. Everything had to be a certain way or we were not approved. Every since I could remember we were all raped at the age of thirteen. Every day of the week would be someone else's day to sleep with our father. I was thirteen years old for two years alone; being forced to perform both vaginal and anal sex almost every night. He continued this pattern of abuse with my sister's once they were of age. All of them.

My father's abuse has lasted over 20 years. At his death no one ever knew the type of person my father was. We did. I stayed with my father and kept his secret until the day he died.

LITTLE GIRL IN ME

The little girl has seen it all
the rapes the beatings, the blood on the wall
the anger the hurt, the drugs the pain
black heart, no soul, no fun, no ran.

Trapped in fear, sorrow and discus,
misguided and mislead to be lost in the dust
because she was broken I could not grow
I want to pass the life of what I've known.

I tried to show her a brighter light
a purpose of living life after life
bigger dreams and longer days
it's finally fun to play in rain
make peace with myself eternally
to free the little girl in me.

PROMISCUOUS

Everyone in the neighborhood called me a whore. In the morning I would skip school and find someone to have sex with for money. All day long I would do the same thing. All week long I would look for money and sex. I was a young prostitute. I love the money, though I loved having sex even more.

It seemed I would get this feeling and I would just enjoy having sex. It didn't matter who I was having sex with as long as it was all the time and it was good. Sex stayed on my mind.

Sometimes I think about the many times I have had sex, including the times my father was raping me, and I laugh. I laugh, however I cry. I'm sad. Sex is my favorite hobby. To me there is nothing like it. Until I figure out why I like it so much I guess I would continue the same pattern, even though I feel there has to be something better.

WHAT'S YOUR PROBLEM

I'm promiscuous
I bite my nails
lick my panties
cut my hair
they say I lie
I bend the truth
talk to myself
I am short fused
I'm always stealing
I cannot cook
love dancing, singing,
writing books
wet the bed till I was nine
day dream till my day rewinds
play with my body
I don't have friends
I hit you once
I'll do it again
my heart is guarded I wont be used
I was mad this way
I was abused.

I DON'T KNOW WHY
(I CANT STOP)

I use to prostitute for my mom,
got addicted, young and dumb
started tricking for myself,
work so much could see my wealth
found a way to support my habit,
out there alone no extra baggage
if I don't work cant feed my nose,
cant smoke my crack so I don't dose
I work my body something serious,
money to be made, and I will get it.

Car is paid off, closet packed,
bills are paid, money stakes
picture perfect one more notch,
got my cocaine and my rock
headed out to work the block,
I don't know why
I just can't stop.

CRACK BABY ANNA

Working the infant intensive care unit was agonizing. The amount of crack babies had tripled since last summer. During a busy week a baby was brought to us from a rural neighborhood in the city. Her mother had given birth to her a few minutes before she was stabbed in a street fight. The baby was about three months premature and addicted to crack cocaine. Her mother was dead before she reached the hospital. We named her Anna.

Anna was three pounds, one ounce. Snow white, no hair and a crack addiction. Anna could almost fit into the palm of your hand. We gave her the best room; room six, the one with the view. Anna was also H.I.V positive. We treated her for her infections as well as her addiction. Thought I was head nurse over the entire unit, I never wanted Anna alone. I was always their. Her mother had died no father, no questions. Four months had past and she was still fighting for her life. She had almost doubled her weight and was starting to move. Her breathing machine and I.V was still necessary.

Anna was special. Even on my off hours I would come in the hospital and pray for Anna. I really wanted Anna to get better. Although there were many babies in Anna's situation, she came in by herself and she would leave by herself. Her mother had died on the city sidewalk in the blizzard cold. Two weeks later Anna died. Anna's death hurt me. We thought we could save her life at least for Anna's mother.

Anna's and her mother's death reminded us about the on-going epidemic steaming from drug abuse, addictions and prostitution. These babies have not, and will not stop coming in. We must give them all our love, for as long as they are in the unit. Room six has already been filled.

SMALL STUFF

Rising stars, bundles of dreams,
too much for some small eyes to see
born in freedom born in pain,
born in alleys,
some in vain.

love is patient, love is kind,
shattered dreams, destiny's blind.
mistakes are made and rarely forgiving,
don't shell up, must keep on living.

friends will stay, and some will go,
no help with them,
one day you'll now.
open a book,
don't look at the cover,
plant a daisy, pick a clover.
catch a breeze on a windy day
pass some knowledge on your way.

AT FIRST I DID

My senior prom was supposed to be the best night of my life. I was queen and my boyfriend was king. He picked me up that night in a limo. He gave me a bouquet of roses. We look like bride and groom. We took pictures and we were off to the prom.

The prom was great. During the limo ride home, we drunk a little champagne and talked. He started kissing and grinding on me. He pulled up my dress and started licking my vagina. I was nervous.

Afterwards he put on a condom and I really got nervous. He asked was I ready, I said "no". He started to lick my vagina more. A few minutes later he asked was I ready again. I didn't know what to say, I had let him go that far, so I said "yes".

It was over in less than five minutes. He looked at me and told me, he loved me. He looked really happy, so we both smiled and held each other for the rest of the ride.

I COULDN'T STOP

One kiss she didn't stop me
kiss her neck,
she let me go
took her shirt off ,
she didn't stop me
now her panties,
she let me go
pull my clothes off,
she didn't stop me
climb on top,
she let me go
stuck in my penis,
she didn't stop me.

Tried to hold back,
she couldn't stop me
I was caught up,
I couldn't stop it
sex isn't what she wanted,
she let me go,
she let me know.

RUNAWAY

My 16th birthday party had been planned for two months. My best friend and I were having a sleepover. Her name was Marie. Marie lived two apartments down from me. Sometimes she would come over to my house when things were not going right at home, that was almost everyday.

Marie would tell me everything that goes on in her house. Once she told me about her abuse. Marie said that her parents were sexually abusing her. She told me "most of the time it was her dad alone, sometimes her mother would join in". Almost every night Marie was forced to perform oral and anal sex. She said "at first she would yell and scream, after a while she got used to it and layed in silence".

When her mother would rape her, she would use candlesticks, sometimes two at a time. Marie said" her mother would like to see her in pain". "It would hurt me" she said. "They hurt me". "They have always hurt me". By this time she was crying, and then she got up and left.

Morning came and I went to her house, her mother answered the door and said that she had run away. I tried to look thru the house and she slammed the door.

My party had came and passed and Marie was nowhere around. I went to her a few days later and Marie was still not there. I didn't see her at school. I wanted to tell someone what Marie had told me. Her parents said she had run away, I kept wondering if something else had happened to her. I never saw Marie again. I guess I will always wonder if she had really run away, or something had happened to Marie. Either way, I will always remember Marie and will always wait on my friend to return.

SAW TOO MUCH

There's nothing that I haven't seen,
before I turned the age thirteen.
my first hustle selling weed,
on the corner of casualties.
moving ounces of cocaine,
older ones schooled me to the game.
flossin is nothing for me,
my house, my car, has gangster beam.
major money, crispy clean,
grill on gleam, a platinum team.
smoke my weed, I pop my pills,
get on raw that's how I chill.
still ain't made no time for slipping,
everyday somebody's missing.
people get killed in your face,
trail is cold without a trace.
born in misery, no way out
trigger happy in a drought.
pistol pulled nowhere to flee,
shot by bucking a robbery.
letting shit go is less than G,
that's why I always carry heat.
I guess I saw too much for me,
no parents, no love,
just me and the streets.

MY TYPE OF GUY

Family members called me crazy. I have been married for almost five years into a life of abuse. My husband and I had gotten married right after high school. My husband and father were just alike. My father was a mental abuser. He would yell a lot and call me names. My husband is the same way.

My husband likes to embarrass me in front of other people. Once he cursed me so bad that I broke down crying in the middle of the street. He always made me feel less than a woman. Everyone noticed his abuse including friends and family. He was an angry man. I made excuses for him, just as my mother did for my father. I was good at making excuses.

My husband was my father. Over the years I have learned to adjust. It would be my father that I see in my husband. Whatever it is, it has taken control over me. I am afraid of him; the same way my mother and I were afraid of my father. I keep quiet most of the time and be careful how I look at him. Hopefully one day I would get the courage and the strength to leave; or I would just wait on peaceful times.

IM USE TO YOU

Tell me I can't
I'll show you I can
tell me I can't
it's better again
say that I didn't I'll show you I wont
say that I do
I'll show you I don't
put me down
I'll teach you the truth
pick me up
that's harvest for you
hold me hear
it's best you don't try
hold me down
you can't you know why
attempt till you realize
what's obviously true
you're callous and abusive
I'm use to you

I LOVE HIM

I still love him, I let him stay,
innocence lost so we must pray.
uncontrollable feelings,
what we'll we do,
if he hurts her again
that's shame on who?
he bought her gifts
we talked for a while,
daddy came back to make us smile
I know he won't touch her
he made us that promise,
if something should happen, "you'll tell me, be honest?"
I know your heart sweetheart
and life is sometimes that way,
your father loves us
and is back to stay.

ONCE I GOT OUT

I'm currently living in a secluded area; a group home for battered women, in fear of my life. My ex-boyfriend had tried to kill me, like he had done so many times before. This time I had made a promise to god and myself that I would leave him.

When he would beat me, he would beat me really bad. Sometimes he would get so angry that he would pick up things and hit me with them. Once he caved my face in with a marble ashtray, broke my teeth, stabbed me twice and left me for dead.

He would force me to perform sexual acts on his friends. He would watch them rape me and would do nothing. I stayed because I was always in afraid for my life. I could not stand up for myself. I had been abused for so long, that I was use to taking his abuse.

Last time he hit me with a bat almost killed me. I received 29 staples across my forehead. I was in a coma for a week. The hospital, social services, and the police department transferred me to this program, after requesting protection for my life.

I am in fear of my life. My boyfriend's purpose was to install so much fear in me that I would remain afraid of him forever, and it worked. Even after he was tried and convicted, I was still afraid. Maybe I would remain afraid for the rest of my life.

TOO MUCH SEX

Male prostitution had been my job on the streets for 13years. I lived life in the fast lane. I was a street whore. I had been raped, robbed and beat out of my money. I was still working the streets. Money in my area was good for men who sold their body. Money made the streets and the streets made me.

Sex was my only way of getting paid. I contacted many diseases, working the streets. Sometimes we would have unsafe sex, didn't matter. Sex was money.

Years past and I was getting older, the streets had begin to get the best of me. I had gotten infected with the H.I.V virus and it had turned into full blown AIDS. I was admitted to a nursing home for AIDS patience. My skin had fallen off my bones and my bowel movements were uncontrollable. My immune system had completely shut down.

Anything would make me sick. I was dying. The street life had taken its toll on my body. There would be no more work for me. I had nothing left besides and aching body and a memory of the street.

STREETS AFTER HOME

Everything I learned, I learned from home,
men on the streets, men on the phone,
my dad is my pimp, I work with my mom,
my house is a drug zone, trapped in a storm.

Beaten and abused since I could remember,
stand on the corner in the middle of November.
work until you make enough money to sleep,
beaten when drugs aren't right on the street.

Childhood is taken by the life of a whore,
beat to the floor when spreading no more.
packed up my bags and headed for life,
mentally ready, into the night.

no skills, no thrills, no job for me,
back to the streets, there's a job for me.
no trust , no love, no money, alone,
dark on the streets, that I would call home.

SIBLING RIVALRY

It was one late night I should have been sleep, however I was lying on the bed listening to the radio. My older brother came into the room and sat on the bed beside me. He told me that he wanted to have sex with me. I said "no".

He still got in the bed with me and started kissing on my chest. He pulled my nightgown up and stuck his penis into my vagina. It hurt really badly. I cried and screamed for him to stop. He was moving back and forth inside of me. After a few minutes he snatched his penis out of my vagina and start having sex with me anal. I yelled and cried for help no one came. It was a cry unanswered. When he finished, he put his penis into my mouth and semen rain down my throat like warm salty water.

My brother pulled the covers over me and told me to go to sleep. Once I agreed no to tell anyone about what had happened, he left. Though he was finished, I was still in pain.

SOMEONE SHOULD HAVE TOLD HIM

Someone should have told him
not to hurt the one he loves,
to treat her like she's precious
to treat her like a dove
but since no one told him
he thought that he could play
with every single heart
that only passed his way
he used them and abused them
so he could be the man
to show all of his friends
that he had the upper hand
he had so many women
he didn't want to choose
so when he caught a virus
to kill them he would choose
now there world is sad and lonely
dark cold and dim
and the only thing they think of
is why didn't some one tell him.

HE DID IT

I told my mom she said "no",
my sister said it must be a joke.
my pastor told me, I should pray,
my friends told me to run away.
my brother won't stop raping me,
when will I ever get to be free?
I need some help to make him stop,
he always hurt me in the dark.
once I tried to get him caught,
mom wouldn't wake at twelve o clock.

I went to grandmas so she could see,
what my brother had done to me.
at the hospital grandma called my mom,
then she said I know you'll come.
I just wanted you to see,
this child is going home with me.

<u>NUMB</u>

In this spot, passion died
widow's wept
a brother cried
I lay there numb
by his bed
a lover sighed
lustful desire
in her eyes I lay there numb

My fathers hands
daughters naïve
sinless guile, mothers pleads
I lay there numb

Friendly phantom
a child reborn
darkened angel
roses thorns
I lay there numb

SCARRED

I've always had a low self esteem since childhood. When I was young I was burned in the face with boiling water.

My grandparents were both old and strict. Grandma made a whip of switches and leather straps, to beat me with. I was beaten along with my sisters and brothers from generation to generation. Years were long living on the farm.

After a night of drinking my grandfather threw a pot of boiling hot water on my face and neck. I was severely burned. Half of my face and neck suffered from 1st degree burns; I was scarred. I was burned blistered and whipped. Exhausted and beaten, my body still would not die. As I lay on the floor looking at the ceiling, I knew as long as I stayed under my grandfather's roof, I would remain scarred inside and out for the rest of my life.

NO ESCAPE

Dad would beat me, Mom would watch
Bandaged wounds, electric marks
Broken bones and dirty clothes
Busted lips and bloody noses
stitches and staples he's grown to now
made his weapons on his own
full of anger
barely grown
he learned to hate
what he called home
tired and beaten from his last mistake
he contemplated a better way
leave them dead or hear to stay
death would be my only escape.

DEATH BY SUICIDE NOTE

My brother was sixteen years old and depressed. My father beat us all the time. He would beat him worse. Dad would also do sexually things to him. Sometimes I could here my brother screaming and hollering for my father to stop. My brother would tell me that dad would have sex with him using bottles and other objects. Once he stuck a broom stick in his anus and made him stand in the middle of the floor.

Dad kept us away from our brother. We were not allowed to talk with him. We could barely see him. My brother would run away and the police would bring him back home. Things had gotten worse every time he returned.

One evening my father found a suicide note on the table; my brother was going to kill himself. "Does this belong to you?", as he walked into the room where my brother was at. When my brother looked at him he swung the bat and hit him in the head. Over and over he beat him repeatedly with the bat. The thought of my brother killing himself angered my father.

My father had found the suicide note and beat my brother to death. My brother lay dead on the room floor, with his head smashed in. My father came out and asks "if anyone else felt like dying"? We all said "no." That was the way my brother felt, and that's what my father did, killed him.

NO DRINKING AGE

The bottomless pit was in the middle of the woods. The kids cut a path, so we could get their faster. The pit was an old dry wishing well. We would gather around it drinking and making wishes. Sometimes we would have cigarettes or pot. We would always have out liquor.

Sometimes we would get really drunk and the older boys would play games with us. They would tell us to take off all our clothes, while they watched us. At times they would have sex with us. The news ones would out up a fight; the older boys would not resist; afraid of getting beaten, or kicked out of the club. Most of the time they would want oral sex, or to play with each other's penis.

When it was all over we would walk out of the woods together, like we usually do; as if nothing happened. We would be hugging and drinking the last of our bottles.

NOT MY SON
(Innocence Lost)

May 13, 2005 I was issued a warrant for my son's arrest. The charge was sexual battery. Police rushed into my house and grabbed my juvenile son out of my arms. I was told that I could come pick him up from the police station. I waited in the visiting room, while my son was charged, booked, fingerprinted and processed into the system.

Later that evening my son was released into my custody. We talked about the accusations being made against him; he denied them all.

Weeks had gone by and I never again received a call from the detective, counselor police officer, or any other government official, to confirm or deny the charges. It seemed as if it had all went away.

Even though it was over I could not forget the way we felt, the cold shoulders, the laughter, the gossip, the mean mugs, and the separation; from one allegation to another. Rumors continued to this day. It didn't have to be true, when he was arrested and charged, he lost his innocence.

NOTHING FROM NOTHING

Don't have a job,
Don't have a man
Don't have a dream,
Don't have a plan
Don't have a life,
Don't have a cover
Don't have a dollar,
Don't have a lover
Don't know how to read,
Don't know how to write
Don't know how to live,
Don't know how to fight
Don't know when to laugh,
Don't know when to cry
Don't know when to talk,
Don't know when to die
guess I don't have much,
and I don't know why.

HIGH PERCENTAGE AREA

Working an area called bottom height had gotten deadly. I was a fourteen year old runaway prostitute. The street life quickly trapped me. I was running from a life of sexual abuse, therefore anything I came across was a better situation for me. I ran into a big time pimp on the streets of New York City. He would get all of the boy's money thru the street and we would pay him a percentage and other small favors in return. My money was good and always on time.

He started taking more than I can afford to give him or more than I wanted to give him. He was nasty and greedy. Several times I would watch him beat up other boys, he had never hit me. Whenever his money was not right he would demand more money from everyone, almost all of it. When he started to monitor the money, we were not able to talk to pocket anything. I started doing shows and some side work whenever I could get a chance. Someone is always telling on the street.

I was coming out of my apartment building, when my pimp slaps me across the face with a pistol. He was yelling for the money and I was yelling for my life. He continued to beat me, kick me, and stab me. I was stabbed a total of eight times and shot two times in the chest. I was then left for dead.

There wasn't anymore working for me. I stayed in the hospital until I was completely rehabilitated. Afterwards I was released to the Department of Children and Families. There I received counseling and treatment, never to return to the streets.

MARKED FOR DEATH

A girl friend of mine and I were runaway prostitutes. We both had escaped a life of abuse and chose the streets over home. We were both young and pretty, and what the streets called ready. I was thirteen and she was fifteen, we were living an adult street life.

One night we went to a party with a couple of guys and put on a regular show. We figure a few dances, a little sex and we would be back on the streets; to make more money. After the dances, my friend went into the room with one of the guys I stayed in the front.

After a while, the guy came out of the room sweating; he looked over at us and walked out of the door. My friend never came out. I walked towards the door slowly, pushing the door opened with my feet. I saw her lying across the bed strangled. She was dead.

Sometimes I think about her and what happened to her that night. I couldn't blame myself. As bad as I felt about her death I could not cry, or anything. The streets still had me. I had to let her go to survive.

ASK

Why is that girls so shy?
must you look me in my eye
why is that boy so mean?
there's no one here to care for me
Why are you just a whore?
have no money or just a "NO"
Why do they use drugs?
in the open or under a rug
Why do you have sex so much?
Not with you, so what's the fuss
Why don't you like to talk?
I think its best I take a walk
Why is it that you like to fight?
right person haven't made my night
How do I get my due respect?
give some, and see what you get
Again, why don't I care?
is it your pain I must bear?
Why are you asking, do you care?
ASK

ANYONE LISTENING

As a young girl school was a breeze. Elementary and middle school, I always made the honor roll. My walls in my room were filled with plaques trophies and certificates. My straight A's got me into clubs, extra curricular activities, trips, banquets, and new friends. Eighth grade summer was a blast, as I prepared for high school. A lot of things happen to me that summer.

My dad started having sex with me almost every day. I wasn't allowed to work anymore. I could not see my friends. I was never available for anything. When school started back I was with drawn, my grades were poor, I started acting out, I was totally different student. My father kept me home from school a lot. He would rape me all day and night.

A social worker came to my house one day looking for me. My dad wasn't home, I let them anyway. I explained to them that my dad had been keeping me home from school whenever he feels like it. I also told him what my dad was doing to me. The police came out and waited on my dad. I went with the social workers. My dad had almost driven me crazy. I wanted to leave my house, leave my dad, and never return. That is what the authorities allowed me to do. I never returned.

MY HEART CRIES FOR YOU

Called me ugly bald and fat
scarred my legs with leather straps,
tongue is mighty, no defense
mom left me with no confidence.

Said I should have been a boy
or something,
belittled me down to nothing
feelings bottled up inside,
father took away my pride.

A girl told me she had been beat,
a boy told me, he had been raped,
I felt there pain the same way.

RAPED IN CUSTODY

I was brought to the boy's home when I was thirteen years old. My father had been abusing and raping me since I was ten. After three years of abuse I was taking out of the home for good.

I went to live in a boys home on the other side of town. One night two of the staff members and one of the boys took me into a dark room. One of the boys made me suck his penis. While the staff members held me down one of the other boys was sticking a broom stick in my butt. I was trying to get away; they held me down and started beating me. The anal rapes and beatings lasted for hours. They all took turns raping me, beating me and putting semen, into my face. The staff member came in and thru me into the shower and then into the bed.

The rest of the night I lay in the bed nervous thinking about the attack. In the morning I went to the group homes nurse and told her what happened to me. After an examination, she immediately called the police. I gave them all the information, including the names of the staff members. I was then placed somewhere I was to receive help and medical treatment. I was sent to a place where I would not be in fear, a place where I am wanted; somewhere I feel safe. Would this be the place, for more trauma or love?

RAPED

They bought me here away from home,
said what my dad, had did was wrong.
tied me to the bed one day,
he raped me on a quiet day.
my had died just two years back,
that's when my day start smoking crack.
he had never hurt be before,
I told the teacher behind closed doors.
I talked to someone with a badge,
said they were going to talk to dad.
doctors told me to lay still ,
pictures and a stitch to heal.
you will be sleeping here today,
going to a special place.
special place for boys your age,
living arrangements have been made.
you wont have to be alone,
or never have to go back home.

KIDS DOWN THE STREET

The kids down the street were severely neglected. Their mother was a crack head prostitute. The children were covered with dirt and their clothes were completely soiled in body waste. One of the girls had sand sores up their entire leg and hair was out to the scalp. The kids basically took care of themselves. One of the older girls was very promiscuous. She was young prostitute. The girl and her mother basically did every thing together; from pulling tricks to boosting, they even shared a crack addiction.

The lights were out in the house they had been out for almost a month. The children were eating out of cans and was bathing outside, using the water hose. The house was infested with roaches and rats. Social Services received a neglect call. Someone had reported abuse.

Social Workers arrived to a horrific scene. The kitchen had dishes stacked across the counter, the lights were off, the children didn't have on any clothes and two of them were eating dry beans and bread on the floor. There were clouds of smoke in the air. As the police and social workers headed towards the back they were surrounded by clouds off smoke and complete filth. The smell of urine wreaked the halls like foul perfume. Rats crossed their feet while walking thru the maze of dirty clothes and boxes.

The kid's mother and older sister were found in the back room smoking crack. Since the girl was only fifteen, their mother was arrested for contributing to the delinquency of a minor and child abuse. The children were taken to the hospital for medical attention and released to the department of children and families.

Hopefully these children can find a loving home where they can receive the attention they need. Without the call to social services, the children may have never survived.

SPIT FIRE

Whorish and charming as they come,
prostitute and local bum
buried in bottle of rum,
I'm just like my mom.

Quick to anger, kind of rude,
nonchalant attitude
very rarely in a good mood,
I'm just like my brother.

Rub my nipples suck my thumb,
rock back and forth slightly shunned,
I'm just like my sister.

Mean and malice,
cruel and hard
tone could rip your heart apart,
feared and ruthless
considered bad.
I'm just like my dad.

SHE SOLD ME

Our walk home takes usually an hour,
this time the detour we took went sour.
the car pulled up, she had flagged down,
she said he's yours this time around.
get in the car and just have sex,
do me this favor and we can rest.
the man in the car was bald and old,
looks and says come out the cold.
at your age I'll be a few minutes,
you may not know yet, this is business.
I got in the back seat and spread my legs,
to late to cry, to late to beg.
in a couple of seconds, he say's it's over
I'm done hear; go back to your mother.

A CONSTANT REMINDER

I've been admitted to the asylum for six years. I am nineteen years old. At age thirteen I tried to commit suicide by slicing my wrist. My father had been anal raping me for years and I could no longer take the abuse. I told my mother at first it seemed as if she didn't believe me, because the abuse went on. Night after night he would rape me. One night my mother caught him and he left the house. Still flashes of abuse would play in my mind.

I could see my father on top of me, sticking things in me. I would wake up shivering. One night I was lying on the coach and someone was having sex with me really hard. I couldn't breathe felt as if I was gasping for air. My arms felt pinned down and so did my legs. I was being raped in my sleep. I felt someone shaking me and I jumped out of my sleep. It was my mother. When I woke up she was standing over me screaming and crying for me to wake up. I told her about the flashes and dreams; she decided to take me to the doctor. The doctor kept me for treatment.

At first the flashes were only at night, I begin to get them during the day. Medication calmed me down afterwards. However, because of the flashes the abuse stayed on my mind. Never being able to fully rehabilitate, I am constantly trying to end my life. Maybe one day the flashes and dreams will stop or my life will end. Either way I will finally be free from my father's abuse.

ASYLUM

Victims of incest abuse and neglect
Mental illness world rejects
Weekly meeting cold restraints
Padded walls, wired gates
Nurses checking
Up my meds
Frantic screaming
Living dead
Raging nightmares
Seeing ghost
Blurry vision overdose
Suicides, runaways
Hypochondria, whorish ways
Families gone
No one to fend
All admitted in a bin

LATCH KEY LIFE

My childhood life I stayed secluded,
unaided thoughts, unnatural illusions,
demented feelings deeply rooted.

Adolescence left in mourning,
lonely night extended till morning,
grief and pain in tears I'm showing,
thought of suicide is growing.

Teenage life of solitary,
bare existence, worn and weary,
too much for my soul to carry.

Adult life I remain apart,
continued pattern from the start
sever anguish rarely shown,
barren life that I have known
I'm used to being alone,
I'll die alone.

LAST TRY

Aspirins, guns, car, or blade
which one will I try today?
I must leave this place, the voices the walls
the touching the kissing, the cringe of it all,
it's just me against them
my family that is,
four men and just me
taking my meds.

They've all taking there turns
vaginal and anal,
oral and mental
I'm not sustaining,
I tried to stop and block the pain
nothing there to block the way,
the gun won't click
the car won't start,
blades aren't sharp
pills won't pop.

Nightfall approaching
in my prayer I would cry,
I can't get the job done
just trying to die.

TAKE A LOAD OFF

Martin was the community drunk. He lived two trailers down from my wife and I. He had two teenage boys. The boys were bad though everyone knew that they were acting out. The boys were severely abused and neglected. Their father martin and their mother were both drunks and couldn't manage.

Standing in the courtyard you could here the boys, yelling and screaming. They were always getting beat. Sometimes Martin would come out with handcuffs, every weekend.

The boys would come over some time and we would talk. Most of the time, they were busted and bandaged up. My wife would see to them and make sure they had something to eat. She loved them.

The night I called the ambulance one of the boys were bleeding bad. His head was gashed open you could almost see thru it. Martin had gotten drunk and hit him with a brick. He was arrested.

Till this day, whenever the boys need me, I have always been there. Sometimes it takes knowing where a person has come from or even knowing where a person has been for you to understand them. The boys know that they are always welcome into my home.

DISPLACED ANGER

My son comes home, barely leaves
take what he wants, take what he needs.
he goes thru my clothes
black eyes, bruised nose
he wrecked both the cars
flipped the kitchen table
broke all the windows
terrorized the neighbors
uses hard drugs
no love is shown
I stay in my room
till my husband comes home
it's safe to say
I am a prisoner at home.

Fear of my life keeps me this way
try not to panic, get thru the day
the violence start
I beg and plead
why is my son so angry at me?

LONELY NIGHT

911 dispatched a call to my unit (child sex crimes). The caller says a child had been raped. The young lady had come home from work one evening and her child had been raped. The little girl had been left with her mother's boyfriend. The child was four years old. She had been raped and left on a bed in the master bedroom. The child was taken to the hospital for medical treatment.

The child's mother was taken into custody and questioned about the child. The mother insisted that the child's father had something to do with anything that had happened. Once he had been found he was questioned. The child's father said that all he could remember was getting high on cocaine and the baby crying. He stated that he might have done some things that he was sorry about he wasn't sure.

The child's mother was charged with rape, neglect, and child abuse. The mother would have to deal with social services about the child. In my unit far too many babies, children, and adolescence, are being raped and abused. It is our job to get the rapist and the abuser off the street and out of the life of the children.

LITTLE WHORE

Mom would leave me thru the night,
my step dad and brother, I'm left to fight
it seemed to me and endless war,
each time meaner than before
limping body tired and worn,
frail and sluggish, I've become
wooden bats and iron poles,
splintered skin, a hand to fold
they rape me till my stuff was sore,
or beat me till I took no more
rubbing alcohol in my wounds,
said the salt to help it sooth
I cry for my father, a cry left ignored,
step dad yells fearlessly, my little whore
fainted, unconscious, dead to the core.

FOSTER HOME

I grew up in a foster home owned by Ms. May. She was an older lady. Ms. May loved kids. Good ones, bad ones, me. My mom was killed on the streets and I never knew my dad. I was neglected by my aunt after my mom died. I went to live in a foster home. There were two other victims of incest and a few kids that had been abused as well. All of us had been taken away from what we called home.

Ms. May loved us all. We would go somewhere every weekend. We went on vacations and trips all the time. We were a family.

I lived with Ms. May until I went off to college. It was a four year University. Leaving my foster home was a hard thing for me to do. Ms. May continued to receive more and more children in her home, raising responsible adults. My senior year of college, Ms. May died.

Ms. May was the best foster parent we could ever have. She loved every kid that walked thru her house, the same. I could feel the love when I returned.

DISAPPEAR

My dad has sex with me,
my mom does too,
once dad chocked my neck till blue.
puts me on the video tape,
every Saturday, uncle Ake.
oral sex, I'm forced to perform,
all since I've been in this home.

My life is better when I run,
they keep finding me and bring me home.
it's dark and cold the saddest of songs.

I stay locked in, three meals of day,
my room in the basement,
since I can't seem to stay.

I can't run anymore,
there is no where to hide,
I'm locked in now, broken my pride
everything is routine
sex, sweat, and tears,
after it's all over, I'll just
disappear.

HOME

Age seven was a touch and feel
early bloom a flower still
eight years old my cousins mist
just a finger, harmless risk

extension cords and leather belts
missing teeth, pain is felt
terror shock and hunger pains
sacrifice my soul for rain

turning twelve it makes me cringe
my dad will take his turn again
will my mother join this time
adjusted to the days and times
delivering me back to face
what once was pain I could not take
confused and left with what is rape?
Another try at me today

One more touch I'm out the door
Im fourteen now I say no more
this time I'm gone, I'm on my own
my mind, heart, and souls at home

IT WASN'T SEXUAL

Last year I worked for a department store. I was sixteen years old. As soon as I started there, it was tension on my job. I requested a meeting with my boss. I told him about the harassment in detail and he assured me that I would not have this problem again. The next day, I went to work things had not changed. Coworkers and now, even the boss had started to harass me. I wanted to quit. I could not understand the personal problem, which they had with me. I made another call.

This was the second meeting with my boss, this time his boss joined us. I told them I had asked to be left alone, and both my boss and coworkers ignored my request.

I was then told since I wasn't getting along with my fellow co-workers, I was fired.

I almost cried. Due to them not wanting to stop the harassment, I was no longer employed. I left that day knowing that I did all I could do to stop the harassment. Maybe they moved on to the next person, I wasn't sure. One thing I was sure of, is that I was no longer a victim.

MY BOSSES OPTION

He said that I had failed a test
I already should have known the rest
cameras caught me stealing cash
last time was suppose to be my last.

he told me to wait there in the office,
getting fired and this is obvious.
he walked in an held a tape,
"stealing again, brave I must say
I am not shocked I must admit
what position do you think I'm in
I'm going to offer you to options
oral sex or get to walking"
he pulled his pants down near his feet
said "what did you expect this time
you thief"
its in my best interest to do what you say
I guess I'll keep my job today.

ANYTHING MISSING

My sister's daughter moved in with me after the death of her parents. Her parent's were both killed in a home invasion. We sat down and on the bed and talked about the do's and don'ts and what I would be expecting from her.

I asked her how she was taking the death of her parents; she smiled and said "oh I'm just fine now. My niece told me that her parents had abused her.

For almost five years, up until there death, they both had been having sex with me. Every night I had been forced to sleep in their bed and perform sexual acts. I was in constant pain and agony. The violence and the beatings were unbearable.

Then she told me her dad had held her down, while her mother burned her in the back with and hot iron. When she lifted up her shirt and showed me the burn mark I was in tears. There was nothing I could do or say. She was so young and bruised inside and out, I wanted to take all the pain and inflict it on myself.

My niece said that "a murder was a terrible way for them to die, however I am glad that it is all over". I assured her again that she is safe with me and that I loved her. I made a promise to my niece that day that I would protect her for as long as I could.

<u>WHY</u>

Why does my sister lick me?
Why does my dad enjoy?
Why doesn't my mom care?
Why didn't he choose the boys?
Why am I ugly?
Why am I so mean?
Why don't I have friends?
Why don't I gleam?
Why can't I sleep?
Why am I mad?
Why am I crying?
Why eat when I'm sad?
Why am I on drugs?
at my wrist with this knife?
What is I can't get over?
Where is my life?

COACH

My basketball coach kept us after practice to wash cars, for a fundraiser at school. We were raising money for high school homecoming. The day started off nice. We all received our assignments and instructions.

My coach called me into his office, told me to bring the money my team had made for the day. When I entered his office he closed and locked the door behind me. Coach turned to me and said sit on the table. He started to take off my clothes, I couldn't move. "Relax" he said, while taking off his pants.

Coach begins to lick on my private parts and rub his fingers across my vagina. Coach was moaning and saying crazy things. I was only in the 9th grade. After he finished licking on me, he stuck his penis into my mouth; it tastes like salt. He left it in my mouth moving it all around, while holding on to my head. Coach continued to do that until semen came out.

Afterwards he told me to put back on my clothes and go outside. I did what the coach asked, and walked out of the door. I never told anyone what the coach did or how I felt, even the coach.

WHY'D YOU ASK?

Did dad touch you?
"NO"
Lick you?
"NO"
Hug you real hard?
"NO"
Play with your hair?
"NO"
Rub on your private?
"NO"
What about your breast?
"NO"
Did he stick his penis in?
"NO"
Not even in you anus?
"NO"
Use his finger?
"NO"

Why'd you ask?
he does those things to me

Year after year more children are fallen victims to abuse. There has been mental, physical, sexual abuse and neglect. This abuse epidemic has wrecked the lives of our youth, and hindered there mental capabilities.

Is the problem our society? Generational curses? Perverted fantasies? Or is it just Drug abuse? No matter how it is developed or perceived, abuse has a negative impact on our nation's children and adults.

These kids in most cases are misguided, uneducated and misunderstood. Promiscuities, anger, uncontrolled behaviors both mentally and physically are all signs of an abuse child. It is important that we see these signs and deal with these issues as they come.

It is also important that we as a society deal with this abuse epidemic, issue by issue, situation by situation, child by child and crisis by crisis.

There is nothing we can do about the children already lost to the hands of an abuser, or to the hard core life of the streets. We have to ask, how can we eliminate the problem? Where do we start? What can we do to insure that there will be stable adults in the future? Will and how will these cycles of abuse end?

ABOUT THE AUTHOR

Jessica Roberts is writer from Orlando, Florida. Jessica has been writing poems and short stories for years. Her style and method of writing has been used to reach all audiences. Jessica's poems and short stories are unique and original; they are all in detail and deliver a serious message. Jessica plans to continue to deliver good reading material for her readers in the future.